very popular books

picture books

Remember the LORD

Colin Buchanan

Welcome to Remember the Lord!

I've had a lot of fun making this book for you. Every page takes the truth from one of my songs and gives you things to do and read that will help you think about what God has to say to you through the Bible.

A grown up might like to sit and read this with you. After you've looked at each page, you can read a short verse or two from the Bible and pray together about what you've learnt. You might even like to read it with me by putting on the CD that comes with the book. There are a few of my other songs on the CD for you to enjoy, too. (All the songs in this book are from my CD called "Remember the Lord".)

Oh, and one more thing! I have hidden Little Colin with his guitar all over the place. Can you find him?

Remember the LORD!

Colin

P.S. Special thanks for lots of hard work, help and encouragement to my Chief Colour-in-er-er and good friend, Geoff R Thompson.

www.colinbuchanan.com.au

The One and Only God

The world is an amazing place, isn't it? There are tall, tall mountains.
Waterfalls tumble down, down, down. Little streams become mighty rivers.
Wide blue-green oceans stretch as far as you can see. There are lands of snow and
ice, lands of desert sand and hot, hot sun. There are thick, green forests, grassy
hills, rocky plains, beaches, lakes, cliffs and valleys. The Bible calls the world
"creation", because it was created—or made—by the ONE and ONLY GOD.
He just spoke, and there it was! Imagine that! "Let there be... Land! Light! Sun!
Stars! Oceans! Plants! Animals! Fish!" All made by the power of His word.
What a MIGHTY, WISE and WONDERFUL GOD!

Are these places in GOD's WORLD _hot_ or _cold_?

PROVE IT!

Q. Who made every thing?
A. God made all things! PROVE IT!

Genesis 1:1
"In the beginning, God created the
heavens and the earth."

READ THE BIBLE
*God Made
the World!
Genesis 1:1-2:3*

SING
*The One
and Only
God*

Let's Pray

O God, your creation is SO amazing! You are the one and only,
powerful and mighty King who made it ALL! We thank you
and praise you, great God, ruler of everyone and everything! Amen!

My God is So Big

Do you like to make things? Maybe you like to paint? Or draw? Or make sand castles, or build with blocks? Perhaps you like to make up stories and songs. When you finish making something, you can stand back and say, "I made that, it's *mine!*" Well, God can say that about the WHOLE WORLD! He made it, he owns it, it is HIS. The land, the sea, the sky, the animals and plants —and all the PEOPLE—even you and me! Only God can look at EVERYTHING there is and say, "MINE!" No one else can say that but God Himself. What a very, very, very BIG GOD He is!

HOW LONG DID GOD TAKE TO MAKE THE WORLD?

6 DAYS

DAY 1 - LIGHT
DAY 2 - SKY
DAY 3 - LAND SEA PLANTS
DAY 4 - SUN MOON STARS
DAY 5 - SEA CREATURES, BIRDS
DAY 6 - LAND ANIMALS, PEOPLE

PROVE IT!

Q. Who made me?
A. God!
PROVE IT!

Genesis 1:27
"So God created man in His own image, in the image of God He created him; male and female He created them."

Who? made what?

Can you match up the MAKERS with what they MADE?

READ THE BIBLE
The Universe has an Owner.
Psalm 24:1-2

SING
My God is So Big

Let's Pray
O God, I am so small and you are so BIG and STRONG and MIGHTY. Thank you that this is your world and you rule it wisely and wonderfully. It all belongs to you, every bit of it—even me! Help me to trust you—the big, BIG God. Amen.

The Old Black Crow

Most birds are very small creatures, aren't they? And there are so many birds in the world—you could never count *all* of them! Screeching cockatoos, colourful rosellas, tiny finches, flittering sparrows, seagulls and pigeons and...old black crows. Jesus said something amazing about birds. He said that God feeds them and sees them, even when one tiny sparrow falls. And Jesus said that there are creatures much, much more precious to God than birds—PEOPLE! People like you and me! So next time you see a bird, remember God sees and knows and cares for and never forgets His children. Are you his child?

God cares for....

wombat

gekko

kangaroo

people in a plane

man at the bus stop

BUS STOP

flowers

children

motorbike lady

BirdWatching

Can you point to...
the bird with a BIG HEAD? the bird driving a car?
the bird that's running? the sleeping bird?
the bird in the nest? the bird with a yellow crest?
the bird with a LOng neck and LOng legs?

THANK YOU, GOD

What can you thank God for? Think of some things and thank Him right now!

READ THE BIBLE
Who is precious to God?
Luke 12:6-7

SING
The Old Black Crow

Let's Pray

Lord God, it's amazing that you know what is happening with every bird in the world. Thank you that you see and know and care for people, too. Thank you that you sent your only Son, Jesus, to show how deep your love is. Help me not to worry but to remember you, no matter what. Amen!

God Our Father

Can you think of someone famous or important? Maybe you've seen them on the TV. Kings and queens, presidents and prime ministers—they are important people. They are commanders of armies and rulers of nations. Sometimes huge crowds of people wait and wait just to get a little peek at them in the distance. But who is the mightiest Ruler of all? Do you know? Yes! God! He is greater than any king or president. He made and rules over EVERYTHING and EVERYONE. God is so important. Could we ever know someone that important? Yes! All who come to Him, trusting in Jesus alone, He promises to call us His very own children! And that means if we trust in Jesus we can come to the IMPORTANT, MIGHTY, HOLY God as our FATHER! Wow!

PROVE IT!

Q. Why did God make me and everything?
A. For His own glory! PROVE IT!

YA GOTTA PROVE IT!

Romans 11:36
For from Him and through Him and to Him are all things. To God be the glory forever and ever. Amen.

What does a GOOD father do?

Protects

serves

rules

disciplines

teaches

loves

provides

GOD our FATHER does all this PERFECTLY!

READ THE BIBLE
Children of God!
Wow! John 1:12,
Romans 8:16,
1 John 3:1

SING
God Our
Father

Let's Pray
Great God, thank you so much that I can come to you in faith and become one of your precious children. You are the perfect, kind, mighty Father of everyone who puts their trust in you. Help me to do what you say, and live my life so that people can see it's all about you. Amen.

Nothing Takes God by Surprise

Do you like surprises? Some surprises are nice—things like presents or treats or when special friends just happen to visit. And some surprises aren't so nice—ills and spills, bumps and thumps—things that scare you or hurt you. A surprise is something you weren't expecting, something you didn't know was coming. But think of this: *nothing* takes God by surprise. God made the world and rules the world and He always knows what is going to happen next. The good bits, the bad bits—everything that happens. God is always in it and ruling over all. That's why we say, "God is SOVEREIGN." It means, "God is KING! KING of EVERYTHING!" Lots of things take us by surprise, but NOTHING takes God by surprise.

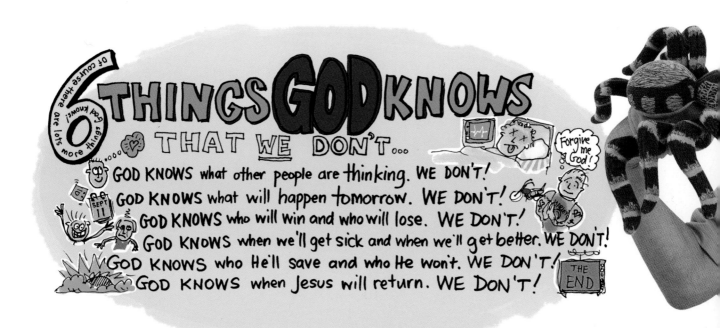

6 THINGS GOD KNOWS THAT WE DON'T...

of course there are lots more things God knows!

GOD KNOWS what other people are thinking. WE DON'T!

GOD KNOWS what will happen tomorrow. WE DON'T!

GOD KNOWS who will win and who will lose. WE DON'T!

GOD KNOWS when we'll get sick and when we'll get better. WE DON'T!

GOD KNOWS who He'll save and who He won't. WE DON'T!

GOD KNOWS when Jesus will return. WE DON'T!

Forgive me God!

THE END

What happens next?

GOOD OR BAD LUCK?

WHAM!

KER SPLASH!

CHEER! HOORAY! CLAP!

SWAN LAKE DISTRICT HOSPITAL — EMERGENCY — AMBULANCE

God wisely rules everything that ever happens - every GOOD thing, every BAD thing. The LORD RULES - not LUCK!

READ THE BIBLE
God rules everything and everyone.
Psalm 33:8-11

SING
Nothing Takes God by Surprise

Let's Pray
O God, I am so weak. I need to eat and sleep, I can get sick, hurt myself and I sin in what I do and say and think. O God, you are so great—you do none of these things. You know—and rule—every single thing that has happened and ever will happen. I'm in so much need of your help to live my life for you, sovereign God! There is nothing better than knowing you!! Amen!

Remember the Lord

Things don't always go the way we'd like them to, do they? Sometimes little, annoying things happen. We might lose a toy, or break something, or take a little tumble or have a fight with a friend. Little, annoying things like that can make us grumpy. We forget God, and we can stop wanting to live His way. And when BIG, SAD, SCARY, DIFFICULT things happen to us, we can forget God and feel like God has forgotten us. But God is always watching and caring for His children. So when things go wrong—no matter what—never forget to always remember to never forget to REMEMBER THE LORD! He always remembers His children!

Have a good look at the things on my tray. Can you close your eyes and REMEMBER all of them? Hmmm....

COLIN

3 TREES OR 3 FACES?
We often see things just one way...
But God sees + plans the whole picture!
(HINT: TURN PICTURE UPSIDE DOWN!)

THE BIBLE GOD'S WORD

Q. & A. When bad things happen to us has God forgotten us? No! God is always watching and working for the good of His children. (Look at Romans 8:28)

READ THE BIBLE
God's good plan for His children—no matter what... Romans 8:28

SING
Remember the Lord

Let's Pray
Great God, there are lots of things that happen that make us scared or sad or grumpy. Help me to know your loving, kind, powerful hand that holds and protects and never ever lets your children go. I want to remember you, day by day, in happy times and sad times, too. Amen.

This is the Gospel

We all like hearing good news, don't we? "It's your birthday!" "I have a treat for you!" "Your best friend is coming over!" "We're all going to play in the park!" They're all good news, aren't they? In the Bible, the word GOSPEL means GOOD NEWS. In fact, it's the happiest news of all: Jesus came, lived a life with no sin, died upon the cross for sinners and rose up from the dead and now He rules forever! Why is that good news for you and me? Well, we're all stuck in the dirty, dark, deadly hole of sin. And only Jesus can get us out! He brings forgiveness of sin and peace with God for ALL who call to Him. JESUS CHRIST takes sinners from DEATH to LIFE—now that's very, very GOOD NEWS!

GOSPEL

Offer: Peace Life
God's Salvation Eternal

Eternal Good News
EXCLUSIVE
JESUS IS GOSPEL

Share the Good News about Jesus!

★ TELL your friends what Jesus has done for you!

He forgave my sins! WOW!

★ PRAY for missionaries—people who share Jesus and serve in other countries!

★ ASK God to help people to see and believe the good news!

★ THANK GOD for the best news of all—JESUS!

READ THE BIBLE
The gospel is Jesus, Jesus is the gospel!
2 Timothy 2:8

SING
This is the Gospel

Let's Pray

Lord Jesus, what a wonder that you save sinners! There's nothing I need more than forgiveness. And that's what you won for sinners when you died on the cross! And what a wonder that you rose from the dead and now you rule all things. Help me to love the gospel and talk about the gospel because it's the best news of all and it's all about Jesus! Amen!

God is So Good

If your Dad gave you a gift, who would you say, "Thank you!" to? Your sister? The bus driver? Dr Dugdale the Dublin dentist? No! You'd thank your Dad, of course, because *he* gave you the gift! The good things in our lives seem to come from lots of different places and lots of different people. But in the end, we only receive good things because GOD decides we can have them. They ALL come from HIM. So if GOD gives us every good thing, who should we say, "Thank you!" to? Yes, we should thank God! Right now, we could say, "Thank you God, for food and friends, music and fun, family, school, the beauty and wonder of your world, the treasures of your love! Thank you, Lord God!" Thank Him again and again and again! No matter what, we always have so much to thank God for!

Can you think of 10 things to thank God for right now?

Think of one for each finger!

Point to the GOOD. Point to the BAD.

SAY THANK YOU for... TO GOD every good thing!

READ THE BIBLE
God and all He does is good! Mark 10:18, Psalm 34:8 & 145:9

SING
God is So Good

 Let's Pray

Good, good God, I thank you for every single good thing, because it all comes from you. Sinners deserve nothing but your anger, but in your goodness you give us so many blessings. And Jesus is the best blessing of all! Help me to say thank you in what I say and in how I live for you. Amen!

God's Map, the Bible

Have you ever been lost? Really, really lost? Maybe you were on a long trip, or a big walk, or at the markets. A wrong turn here, a wrong turn there—and all of sudden you don't know where you are! But... what if you had a map? A map can show you where you came from, where you are and where you need to go. Of course, you need the right map. And you need to know how to read it properly. Well, God has given us a map for our lives—it's the BIBLE. The Bible tells us the safe way, the best way—the ONLY WAY—to Him. If you live by the Word of God and do what He says, God will guide you day by day—and you'll never be lost!

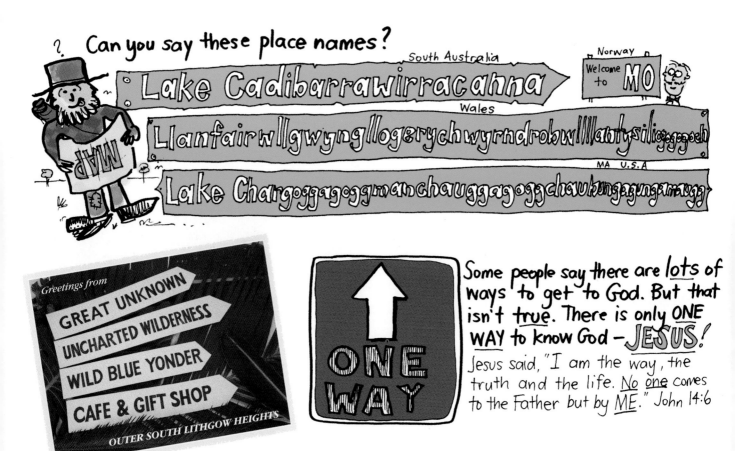

? Can you say these place names?

South Australia
Lake Cadibarrawirracahna

Norway
Welcome to MO

Wales
Llanfairwllgwyngllogerychwyrndrobwllllantysiliogogogoch

MA U.S.A
Lake Chargoggagoggmanchauggagoggchaubunagungamaugg

Greetings from
GREAT UNKNOWN
UNCHARTED WILDERNESS
WILD BLUE YONDER
CAFE & GIFT SHOP
OUTER SOUTH LITHGOW HEIGHTS

ONE WAY

Some people say there are lots of ways to get to God. But that isn't true. There is only ONE WAY to know God – JESUS!
Jesus said, "I am the way, the truth and the life. No one comes to the Father but by ME." John 14:6

Find these on the map!

Guitar house

FIXING DUN QIK & SONS

rope swing tree

castle

rocket

READ THE BIBLE
God's Word shows you the way!
Psalm 119:105 & 25:45

SING
God's Map the Bible

Let's Pray

Lord God, I am so lost without you. I choose bad things to do, I choose bad things to think, I choose bad things to say. I can never find my way to you without your map, your light, your word—the Bible. Please help me to stay on your path. Teach me, for you are God my Saviour. Amen!

Hebrews 1:1-2

Have you been to the library or a big bookshop? Lots of people have written lots of books with lots and lots of pages and lots and lots and lots of words. There are so many books in the world, but the BIBLE is the most wonderful, most precious book of all. Do you know why? It's because God speaks to us through the words of the Bible. God gave the words and people wrote them down and there are NO mistakes in the Bible.

There are TWO main parts of the Bible. In the OLD TESTAMENT, God chose a little nation called Israel and He spoke to them through His messengers, called prophets. In the NEW TESTAMENT, God speaks to every nation through His Son, Jesus. Do you want to know what God says? Do you want to know Him and love Him and serve Him and obey Him? Well, listen to His Word! Listen to Jesus!

"HOW TO..." books

cook books

picture books

very popular books

very old books

story books

School books

Isaiah 53:6

Have you ever seen a farmer rounding up his sheep? Sometimes he uses a dog to help him. He might ride a horse or a motorbike. It isn't easy to get sheep to go where you want them to, because sheep go astray. You want them to go one way and they go the other way. The Bible says people are like that. God says, "Go MY way!" and we just go astray. We all decide our way is better than His way.   Every day, so much of what we do isn't for God or for other people, it's for ourselves. That's sin. And our lives stink of sin.   (Another word for sin is iniquity.) Sin must and will be punished by the sin-less God. But Jesus died upon the cross to save sheepish, straying sinners like you and me. Isaiah 53:6 tells us a deep and marvellous truth: through Jesus, God makes saved saints out of lost, sinful sheep!

We all sin on the...

OUTSIDE
Things we DO and DON'T
DO
LIKE.. FIGHTING LIES
STEALING HURTING
SWEARING GOSSIP

INSIDE
Things we DO and DON'T
THINK
LIKE.. HATING GREED
ENVY LUST
UNBELIEF

Where are the farmer's sheep?

And what are they doing?

Let's Pray

King Jesus, I have strayed like a sheep and in so many ways I go my own way. I want to trust you and turn from my sin. More than anything, I need the forgiveness that is only found in you. I don't want to stray—I want to be yours, faithful, obeying, not easily straying. I need you, Jesus! I need you! Amen.

John 14:1-4

Do you worry? There are lots of things to worry about. Does he like me? Will she forgive me? Will I find it? Is it broken? Can I have it? Will I get better? Are they coming back? Am I lost? Am I too late? Jesus said a very kind and tender thing to His friends, the disciples, when they were worried. He told them to trust Him because He was going to prepare a wonderful home for them in heaven. And he did that by dying on the cross. What happened three days later?   He rose to life! And one day He'll return to take all His friends to share our heavenly home—forever! Sickness, sadness, temptations, disappointments, hard times, sin and death matter so much to Jesus, He is going to end them all one day—forever! While we wait for that time, let's trust Mighty Jesus with all our worries.

GREAT BIBLE WORRIERS

WHO? → worried about... → WHAT GOD DID

Elijah ...being the very last one left in the world who loved God.
★ Told Elijah there were 7,000 (lots of) Israelites who still loved God. ★ Gave Elisha to him as a friend + helper.

Moses ...being too weak and useless to lead God's people.
★ Gave Moses powerful + wonderful signs ★ Gave him Aaron to speak for him. ★ Led God's people OUT of Egypt!

David ...being captured and killed by King Saul.
★ Kept David safe ★ Raised David up to be the great king.

Peter ...being known as a friend of Jesus.
★ God sent His Holy Spirit and made Peter a BRAVE and FAITHFUL apostle (leader of God's people.) WOW!

Today, in some places, followers of Jesus face many hardships and worries because they faithfully follow Him. Will you pray for believers who are hurt and hated because of Jesus? Here are some countries to pray for... INDONESIA India SAUDI ARABIA Afghanistan CHINA

READ THE BIBLE
Jesus saved sinners by dying on the cross.
Mark 15:24-41

SING
John 14:1-4

Let's Pray
Lord Jesus, it must have been so hard to go to the cross to die for sinners like me. Your friends the disciples didn't understand what was happening and your enemies were so cruel. I praise you that you smashed death, rose from the dead and won a way to heaven for everyone who trusts in you—even me! Amen.

Romans 6:23

Do you know someone who goes to work? People work to earn money, to pay for food and clothes and houses and other stuff. The money they work for we call "wages". The Bible says that everyone who sins—and that's everyone of us—is working for wages. But not money. It's death. Every one of us sins and every sinner must die—that's what you get for your sin. The wages of sin is death and hell. How terrible! Is there any escape? Yes! The free gift of God is not death but life—forever and ever, through the Lord Jesus Christ. He got death so that sinners could get life—forever! Which one will you chose? The terrible, deadly wages of sin? Or God's wonderful gift of LIFE in Jesus?

BREAK a window and someone has to PAY to make it right. BREAK God's law by SINNING and someone has to PAY to make it right.

JESUS OR YOU?

What did Jesus say about...

HELL ↓   ↑ HEAVEN

- Hell is punishment for sin. Mt 5:22
- Hell is a place of destruction. Mt 10:28
- God has the power to cast sinners into hell. Luke 12:5
- Hell is like a fire that never goes out. Mk 9:43
- Hell is a place of darkness, weeping and pain. Mt 26:30
- Hell is eternity without God. Mt 25:41

- Heaven is eternal life. Mt 25:46
- Heaven is God's home. Mt 5:45
- Heaven is the home of the righteous. Mt 5:10
- Heaven is a place of treasure and reward. Mt 5:12
- Heaven is a place of never-ending happiness + rejoicing. Luke 15:7 Mt 6:20
- Heaven is eternity with God.

JESUS will say to everyone either "Come to heaven!" Mt 25:34 or "Go to hell!" Mt 25:31-46

READ THE BIBLE
God does not deal with every sinner as they deserve.
Romans 5:6-11

SING
Romans 6:23

Let's Pray

Holy God, I am not like you. You are full of goodness and truth. There's nothing bad in you, but there are no people like that. We all sin and we all disobey and we all deserve the wages of sin—death. Please forgive me. I need your free gift of eternal life in Jesus so, so much. Amen

Revelation 3:20

Have you ever knocked on a door and waited and waited for someone to come and answer it? You might have been at a friend's house, waiting for them to come and open up the door. Knock! Knock! Knock! No one likes to be kept waiting. But imagine doing that to the Lord Jesus! That is what God's people do when they disobey Him, when they forget His word and love other stuff more than Him. So, are you staying close to Jesus today? If you've disobeyed, how wonderful to know that Jesus won't ever forget His friends, even when they forget Him—He comes to His friends, full of forgiveness. Knock! Knock! Knock! Come in, Jesus!

Who lives where?

Christians have an everlasting home in heaven!

Who did Jesus eat with?

tax collectors

lepers (sick guys)

sinners

Jesus said, "I have not come to call the righteous, but SINNERS" Mk 2:17

Colin's home-made KNOCK! KNOCK! Jokes!

Knock! Knock!
Who's there?
Armageddon
Armageddon who?
Arm-a-geddon tired
of waiting here!

Knock! Knock!
Who's there?
Jordan
Jordan who?
Jor-dan-arily
make your visitors
wait so long?

Knock! knock!
Who's there?
Ahab
Ahab who?
A-hab been waiting
for you to open the door!

Knock! Knock!
Who's there?
Priest.
Priest who?
Priest to meet you.
Now open the door!

Knock! Knock!
Who's there?
Joab.
Joab who?
Jo-ab any idea how
long I've been waiting?

Knock! Knock!
Who's there?
Zacchaeus.
Zacchaeus who?
Zacc-hae-us in the door,
can I let myself in?

WHO'S THERE?

READ THE BIBLE
What did God say to a forgetful church?
Revelation 3:14-22

SING
Revelation 3:20

Let's Pray

Jesus, you can do anything you want and it will always be good. I need you to work in my heart to make me love you and your word and your people more. Forgive me for turning my back on you, leaving you out of my life and forgetting you. Come in, Jesus! Come in and make my life all about you! Amen!

Here are the words of the songs featured in this book.

The One and Only God

1. He's the God of the endless outback
   He's the Lord of Kakadu
   He made Mt Kosciusko
   And he made Uluru
   Every mountain
   Every river
   Every waterfall ...
   The One and Only God
   The One and Only God
   The One and Only God made it all!

2. He's the God of the Simpson Desert
   He's the Lord of the Kimberley
   He made the mighty Darling
   He made the Coral Sea
   Every mountain
   Every river
   Every waterfall ... CHORUS

3. He's the God who made the Daintree
   He's the Lord who made Lake Eyre
   He made this land Australia
   His glory's everywhere
   Every mountain
   Every river
   Every waterfall ... CHORUS

My God is So Big

My God is so BIG
So strong and so mighty
There's nothing my God cannot do
That's true!
My God is so BIG
So strong and so mighty
There's nothing my God cannot do
That's true!
The mountains are his
The valleys are his
The stars are his handiwork, too
My God is so BIG
So strong and so mighty
There's nothing my God cannot do
That's true!

The Old Black Crow

1. There's an old black crow
   Sitting in the gum tree
   He's plump and he's well-fed
   A beetle here, a cicada there
   Is the black crow's daily bread
   I think it should be said...

   Chorus
   There's a Lord who cares for the old black crow
   The wombat, the gekko and the kangaroo
   And one thing's sure, we are worth much more
   To the God who cares for people too!

2. Mrs Wombat digs herself a little burrow
   To keep her warm and dry
   It's her home sweet home
   That's she's made her own
   Better than money can buy
   And here's the reason why...
   CHORUS

3. The gekko lives in the sands of the desert
   Where it's very dry and hot
   He's small and frail with a stumpy tail
   But hungry he is not
   All he needs he's got ... CHORUS

God Our Father

God our Father made the trees
to grow and grow and grow
God our Father made the wind
to blow and blow and blow
God our Father made the birds
to fly and fly and fly
Down to fly upon the ground
and up into the sky

Nothing Takes God by Surprise

1. In the beginning God spoke a word
   And that's how the world began
   And every moment 'til the end of time
   Is part of God's wonderful plan

   Chorus
   Nothing takes God by surprise, No-no!
   Nothing takes God by surprise, No-no!
   He is sovereign
   He's in contro-o-ol
   Nothing takes God by surprise

2. In the good bits, the bad bits, in all of your life
   No matter what happens to you
   You can be sure God is always in it
   And Jesus can carry you through
   ... CHORUS

3. He knows every deed before it's done
   He knows your every thought
   There's not one thing that he's left to chance
   That's why we call him L-O-R-D, Lord ... CHORUS

Remember the Lord

1. If you stub your toe when you get out of bed
   And you slip in the shower and knock your head
   If you miss your breaky and your bike tyre's flat
   If the dog eats your lunch and you step on the cat...

   Chorus
   Remember the Lord, Oh-oh!
   Remember that he is in control
   Remember the Lord Oh-oh!
   He's watching his children
   He cares, Oh-oh!
   Remember the Lord, Oh-oh! Oh-oh!

2. If you get to school about half hour late
   And the principal meets you at the gate
   If you can't remember one plus two
   And you're busted for something that you didn't do ... CHORUS

3. If your Dad is crusty and your Mum's in a flap
   And you spill the custard in your sister's lap
   If you're sent to bed and you don't know why
   And you can't get to sleep and you just want to cry ...
   CHORUS

This is the Gospel

1. Remember Jesus Christ
   Raised up from the dead
   In the line of David
   Spotless Lamb of God
   Slaughtered for our sins
   Risen King of kings
   This is the gospel
   Of Jesus Christ

   This is the Gospel
   The risen Jesus
   Taking sinners from death to life
   It's the good news
   Of our salvation
   So remember
   Jesus Christ

2. Remember we were lost
   We were dead in sin
   But by the power of Jesus
   Were made alive again
   And though we may be chained
   The Word of God remains
   The mighty gospel
   Of Jesus Christ ... CHORUS

God is So Good

God is so good
God is so good
God is so good
He's so good to me

God's Map—the Bible

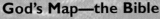

1. Well you're gunna get lost
   And it won't take long
   If you don't take a map
   To Kickatinalong
   You'll be lost in the scrub
   Quick as can be
   If you don't take a map
   To Upper Gumtree

   Chorus
   And if we read God's Word
   We'll know the way
   To live for Jesus and obey
   We'll only know the way to go
   If we read God's Map - the Bible!

2. It's a winding road
   It'll be bad luck
   If you don't take a map
   To Chuckasackamuk
   And if you head outback
   You'll meet your match
   If you don't take a map
   To Hakabadpatch ... CHORUS

Hebrews 1:1-2

In the past God has spoken
To our forefathers through the
   prophets
At many times and in various ways
But in these last days he has spoken
To us by his Son
Whom he appointed heir of all
   things
And through whom the universe
   was made
Hebrews 1, 1 and 2.

Isaiah 53:6

We all like sheep have gone astray
Baa baa doo baa baa
Each of us has turned to his own
   way
Baa baa doo baa baa
But the Lord has laid on him
The iniquity of us all - sing!
Baa baa doo baa baa
Isaiah 53, 6 - UH!

John 14:1-4

John 14, 1 to 4
John 14, 1 to 4

Do not let your hearts be troubled
Trust in God, trust also in me
In my Father's house there are
   many rooms
If it were not so I would have told
   you
I'm going to prepare a place for you
And if I go and prepare a place for
   you
I will come back and take you to
   be with me
That you also be where I am
You know the way to the place
where I am going

John 14, 1 to 4
John 14, 1 to 4

Romans 6:23

Romans 6, 23
For the wages of sin is death
But the gift of God is eternal life
Through Jesus Christ our Lord
A-men-nnnnnnn!

Revelation 3:20

Here I am I stand at the door and
   knock
Rat tat tat! Tat tat tat!
If anyone here's my voice
And opens up the door
I will come in - I will come in
And eat with him - and eat with
   him
And he with me
Revelation 3, 20
Rat tat tat! Open up that door!
Revelation 3, 20
Rat tat tat! Open up that door!

These songs are all
from my CD, 'Remember
the Lord', which is
available separately